With This Ring
A Hammered Dulcimer Collection for Weddings and Special Occasions
Arranged by Jeanne Page

© 2006 BY MEL BAY PUBLICATIONS, INC.
ALL RIGHTS RESERVED. INTERNATIONAL COPYRIGHT SECURED. MADE AND PRINTED IN U.S.A.
No part of this publication may be reproduced in whole or in part, or stored in a retrieval system, or transmitted in any form
or by any means, electronic, mechanical, photocopy, recording, or otherwise, without written permission of the publisher.

Visit us on the Web at www.melbay.com — E-mail us at email@melbay.com

TABLE OF CONTENTS

About the Author 3
Before You Begin 4
About the Tablature 5
A Few Notes 6

Songs
All in a Garden Green 8
Be Thou My Vision 10
Bridal March 12
Carolan's Concerto 14
Carolan's Draught 18
Carolan's Receipt 20
Eamonn an Chnoic 22
Fur Elise 24
Gathering Peascods 26
George Brabazon 28
Grimstock 30
Holy, Holy, Holy 32
Hymn to Joy 34
Jesu, Joy of Man's Desiring 36
King William's March 38
Lady Athenry 40
Lady Owen's Delight 42
Lauda di Maria Madellena 44
Lord Inchiquin 46
Nearer, My God 48
Once I Loved a Mayden Faire 50
Pachelbel's Canon 52
Planxty Burke 54
Si Bhean Locha Lein 56
Spagnoletta 58
Spring: The First Movement 60
The Grenadier and the Lady 62
Trumpet Voluntary 64
Wedding March 66
Wilson's Wilde 68
Y Dydd 70

About the Author

Jeanne Page began her life-long journey into folk music at age 12 singing and playing the guitar. Since then, she has gravitated to focus primarily on the hammered dulcimer and Celtic harp. She teaches both instruments privately and through the University of New Mexico. Jeanne performs solo and with her band "The Next Chapter," and directs a youth harp ensemble called, "The Apple Mountain Harp Kids." She is a co-founder of the "Albuquerque Folk Festival" and served as the Event Director. Jeanne has several instructional books available through Mel Bay Publications including Hammered Dulcimer Chords (MB96675), Arranging for Hammered Dulcimer (MB98121), Irish Songbook for Hammered Dulcimer (MB99711), and Scottish Songbook for Hammered Dulcimer (MB99712). She also has several CD's available, "Time's Gone By," "The Next Chapter," and "The Way or the Road." For more information visit her website at www.thenextchapter.net.

Before You Begin...

This collection includes the following for each song:

- A "melody only" version.
- An intermediate arranged version.
- Guitar Chords.

The melody version can be used in the following ways:

- As a beginning level version.
- As a tool for intermediate players. It is best to practice just the melody and know it well before you begin the arranged version. This better equips you to emphasize the melody and to keep it from being buried in a complicated arrangement.
- When performing a tune, play the "melody only" version the first time through and then the arranged version the second time through.
- As a lead line for other instruments such as fiddle or penny whistle, when playing in an ensemble.
- In a dulcimer club setting, the beginners can play this version, while intermediates play the other.

The arranged version can be used in the following ways:

- As a "stand alone" arrangement.
- As a starting place for advanced players who may choose to add more arpeggios, fills, scale runs, etc.
- In a dulcimer club setting, the intermediate players can play this version while the beginners play the melody only.

The chords are noted above the staff to be used in the following ways:

- For chordal backup on the hammered dulcimer while other instruments play the lead in an ensemble.
- For other instruments, such as guitar, to play backup for the hammered dulcimer lead.

The only exception to the above descriptions is "Pachelbel's Canon." There is only one version of Pachelbel's Canon in the book. The canon is a well-known series of variations which become increasingly complex. Instead of a 'melody-only' version, the beginning player can learn the first two or three variations, and repeat those as many times as is necessary.

About Tablature...

Tablature systems have been created to make a new instrument more accessible to the musician. While many TAB systems accomplish this smoothly and effectively (the mountain dulcimer is a great example), I have yet to see a hammered dulcimer version that wasn't at least as time consuming to learn as standard musical notation. Often it is more challenging! Until some wise and creative person comes up with a system that simplifies the process of learning music on the hammered dulcimer, I will continue to recommend that players learn standard musical notation on the treble staff.

The graph here is intended to help you accomplish this task and to locate the notes you are searching for in the written music. Keep it right next to you when working a song so that you can refer to it often. There are also some wonderful introductory books for hammered dulcimer that explain the logic of the instrument, where different keys are located, etc., which will make the process easier to manage.

Have fun with these tunes—I hope you enjoy them as much as I do!

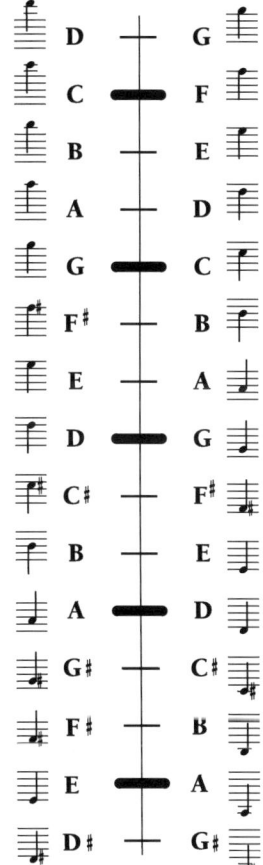
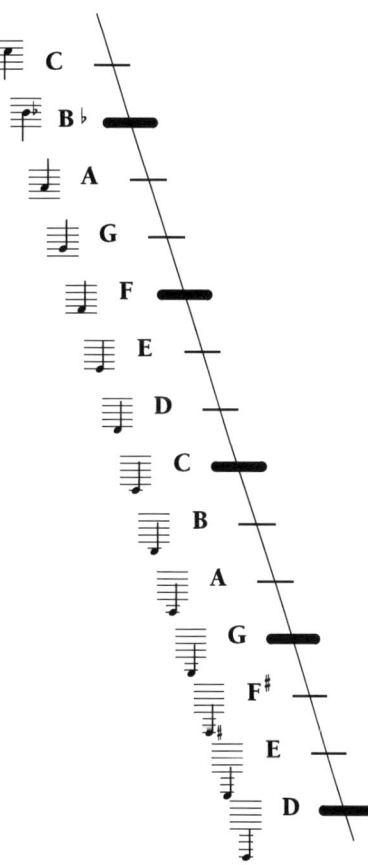

A Few Notes...

If you're looking for additional tunes for your wedding or special celebration, the following are some suggestions that I have used in my own prelude repertoire found in my other books:

From "Irish Songbook for Hammered Dulcimer": Believe Me If All Those Endearing Young Charms; Blind Mary, Carolan's Welcome, Down by the Sally Gardens, Eleanor Plunkett, The Gentle Maiden, Give Me Your Hand, Hewlett, Maggie, Morgan Megan, Planxty Fanny Power, Planxty Irwin, Si Beag Si Mor, Southwind

From "Scottish Songbook for Hammered Dulcimer": Annie Laurie, Flow Gently Sweet Afton, Lassie With the Yellow Coatie, Mairi's Wedding, Tiree Love Song, Wild Mountain Thyme

This page has been left blank
to avoid awkward page turns.

All in a Garden Green

All in a Garden Green

Be Thou My Vision

Be Thou My Vision

Bridal March

Wagner

Bridal March

Wagner

Carolan's Concerto

O' Carolan

Carolan's Concerto

O' Concerto

Carolan's Draught

O' Carolan

Carolan's Draught

O' Carolan

Carolan's Receipt

O' Carolan

Carolan's Receipt

O' Carolan

Eamonn an Chnoic

Eamonn an Chnoic

Fur Elise

Beethoven

Fur Elise

Beethoven

Gathering Peasods

Gathering Peascods

George Brabazon

O' Carolan

George Brabazon

O' Carolan

Grimstock

Grimstock

Holy, Holy, Holy

Dykes

Holy, Holy, Holy

Dykes

Hymn to Joy

Beethoven

Hymn to Joy

Beethoven

Jesu, Joy of Man's Desiring

J. S. Bach

Jesu, Joy of Man's Desiring

J. S. Bach

King William's March

Clarke

King William's March

Clarke

Lady Athenry

O' Carolan

Lady Athenry

O' Carolan

Lady Owen's Delight

Lady Owen's Delight

Lauda Di Maria Maddalena

Lauda Di Maria Maddalena

Lord Inchiquin

O' Carolan

Lord Inchiquin

O' Carolan

Nearer, My God

Mason

Nearer, My God

Mason

Once I Loved a Mayden Faire

Once I Loved a Mayden Faire

Pachelbel's Canon

Johanne Pachelbel

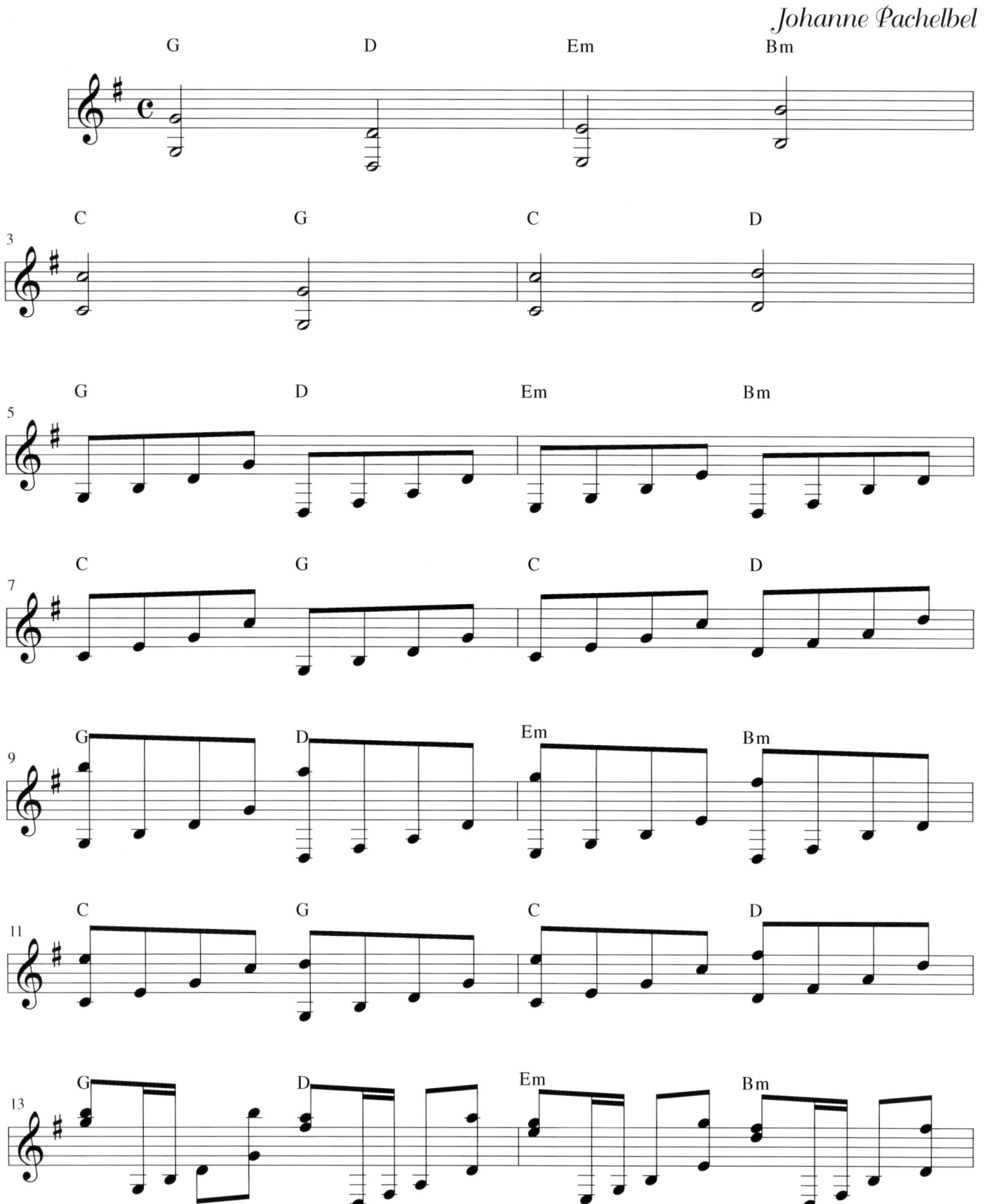

Planxty Burke

O'Carolan

Planxty Burke

O' Carolan

Si Bean Locha Lein

Si Bean Locha Lein

Spagnoletta

Praetorius

Spagnoletta

Praetorius

Spring: The First Movement Theme
From "The Four Seasons"
Vivaldi

Spring: The First Movement Theme
From "The Four Seasons"
Vivaldi

The Grenadier and the Lady

The Grenadier and the Lady

Trumpet Voluntary

Clarke

Trumpet Voluntary

Clarke

Wedding March
From "A Midsummer Night's Dream"
Mendelssohn

Wedding March
From "A Midsummer Night's Dream"
Mendelssohn

Wilson's Wilde

Wilson's Wilde

Y Dydd

Y Dydd